I0818545

WNBA

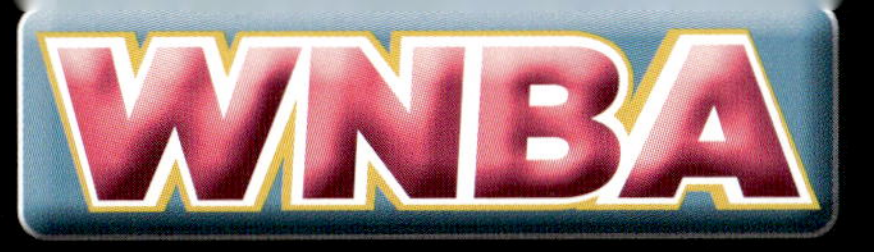

LAS VEGAS ACES

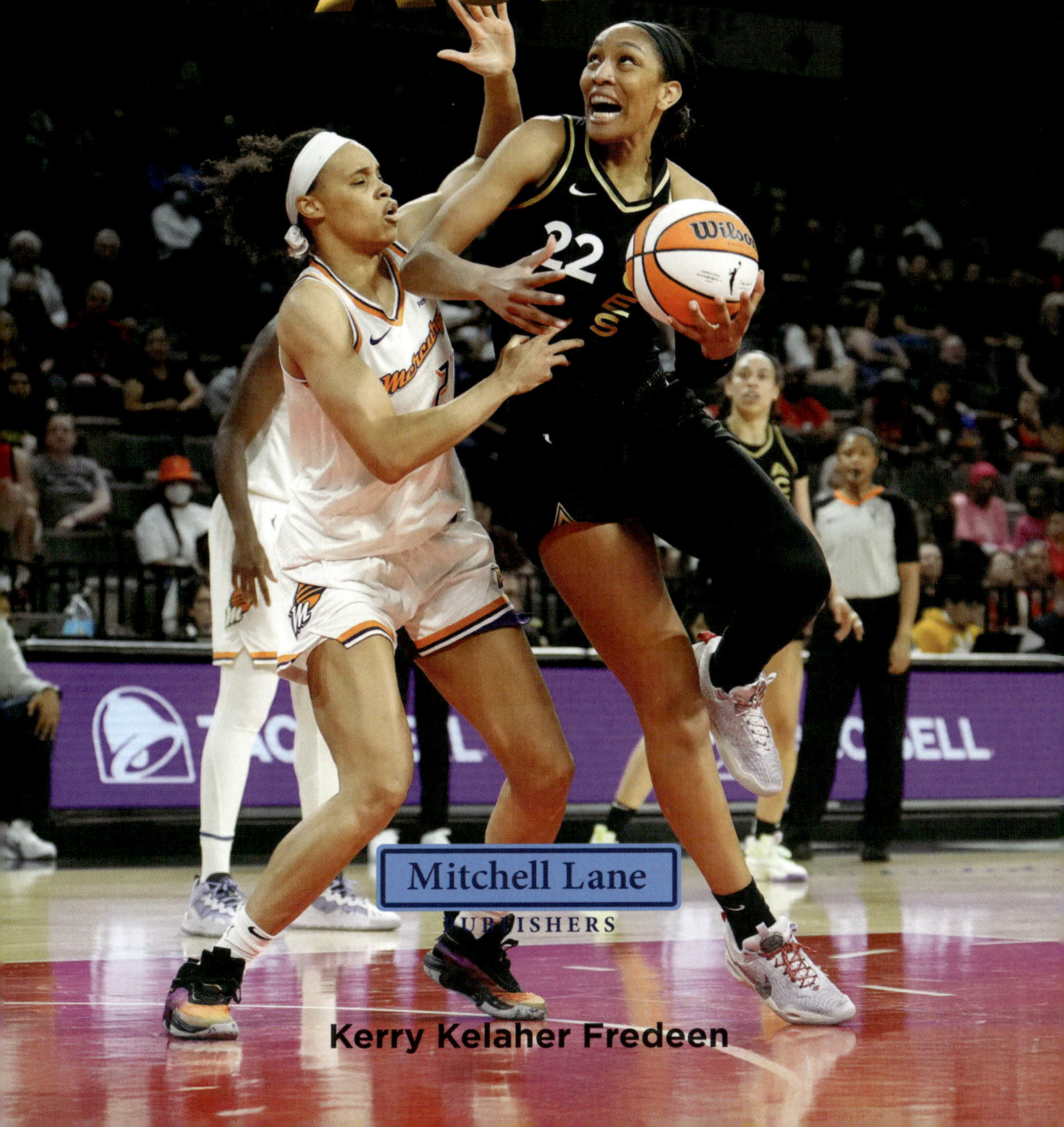

Mitchell Lane
PUBLISHERS

Kerry Kelaher Fredeen

Mitchell Lane
PUBLISHERS

mitchelllanepub.com

2001 SW 31st Avenue
Hallandale, FL 33009

First Edition, 2026.
Author: Kerry Kelaher Fredeen
Designer: Ed Morgan
Editor: Tammy Gagne

Series: WNBA
Title: Las Vegas Aces

Library bound ISBN: 979-8-89260-480-2
eBook ISBN: 979-8-89260-492-5

Photo credits: p. 7, 11, 15 newscom; p. 27 wikimedia; balance Alamy

CONTENTS

Chapter ONE

BACK-TO-BACK CHAMPIONS

BASKETBALL CHAMPIONSHIP

It was October 18, 2023, game four of the Women's National Basketball Association (WNBA) Championship. The Las Vegas Aces were one win away from taking home the title. The team won the trophy in 2022. Only two WNBA teams had ever been back-to-back champions, and the last time it happened was twenty-one years ago. There was a great deal on the line.

CHAPTER ONE

The Aces came into the series with a 34–6 record, the best in the league. But their opponents, the New York Liberty, had an impressive season too, with a 32–8 record. The Aces were ahead in the series, two games to one. The trophy was well within reach if they kept working toward it together.

But the deck was stacked against the Aces. Two of their starting players were on the sidelines due to injuries. **Center** Kiah Stokes and **guard** Chelsea Gray both suffered foot injuries in game three and had to sit out the rest of the finals.

The Liberty got off to a fast start with a 23–13 lead at the end of the first quarter. But the Aces pulled together, led by **forward** and center A'ja Wilson. With just 41.7 seconds left in the game, the Aces were ahead by a single point. They used a timeout to hold on to the lead. With just 8 seconds left, the Liberty got the ball but missed the shot that would have tied the series. Soon the buzzer sounded. The Aces won their second championship in a row.

Back-to-Back Champions

The Aces celebrate their win over the Liberty in the 2023 WNBA Championship.

CHAPTER ONE

Wilson scored 24 points and was named Finals Most Valuable Player (MVP). She gave credit for the win to her teammates. “We fought through so much **adversity** throughout the season. . . . We came out on top. I can’t express how proud I am of my teammates. They picked me up when I was down. We cried together. We prayed together and now we are popping champagne together!” she told reporters at the end of the game.

The Las Vegas Aces began as the Utah Starzz, one of the original WNBA teams in 1997. They had the worst record in the league that first year. But they gambled by making some changes and made their way to the top.

Back-to-Back Champions

FAST FACT

A'ja Wilson has written a book called *Dear Black Girls: How to Be True to You.* It includes stories and lessons from Wilson's life.

Chapter TWO

A TEAM ON THE MOVE

Margo Dydek was the Utah Starzz first pick in the 1998 WNBA draft.

The WNBA began in 1997 with eight teams. Each of them was in a city with a men's National Basketball Association (NBA) team. Located in Salt Lake City, one of the WNBA teams was called the Utah Starzz.

The Starzz got off to a rocky start. They didn't have a winning record until 2000. In 2001 and 2002, the Starzz reached the playoffs but didn't make it into the finals.

CHAPTER TWO

After the 2002 season, the team was sold and moved to San Antonio, Texas. It then became the San Antonio Silver Stars. In 2008, the Stars made it into the league finals at last. They also made the playoffs for the next four years.

In 2014, the team was renamed yet again, this time dropping the word *Silver* from its name. The San Antonio Stars went through a rough patch, with the worst record in the league between 2015 and 2017. They didn't win more than eight games in any of those seasons. But their luck was about to change.

In 2018, the team was sold again and moved to Las Vegas, Nevada. The Stars were renamed the Las Vegas Aces at this time. Coach Bill Laimbeer told the *Swish Appeal* website, "Selecting a new name is an important and symbolic step. We have a strong **roster** driven to succeed, which makes this name an ideal choice. 'Las Vegas Aces' is a nod to the excellence, confidence and competitive spirit of our new hometown."

A Team on the Move

Coach Bill Laimbeer led the Aces to the playoffs three times.

CHAPTER TWO

The move to Las Vegas **revitalized** the team. With their new name and city, the Aces returned to their winning ways. They reached the playoffs again in 2019. And in 2022 and 2023, they became back-to-back WNBA champs.

The Aces were grateful for their new home and fans. The players wanted to give back to the community that had welcomed and supported them. With the Aces Care School Tours, the team began visiting local schools to talk to young people about the value of education and **literacy**, as well as the power of kindness.

FAST FACT

The Aces were the first professional sports team to win a championship for Las Vegas.

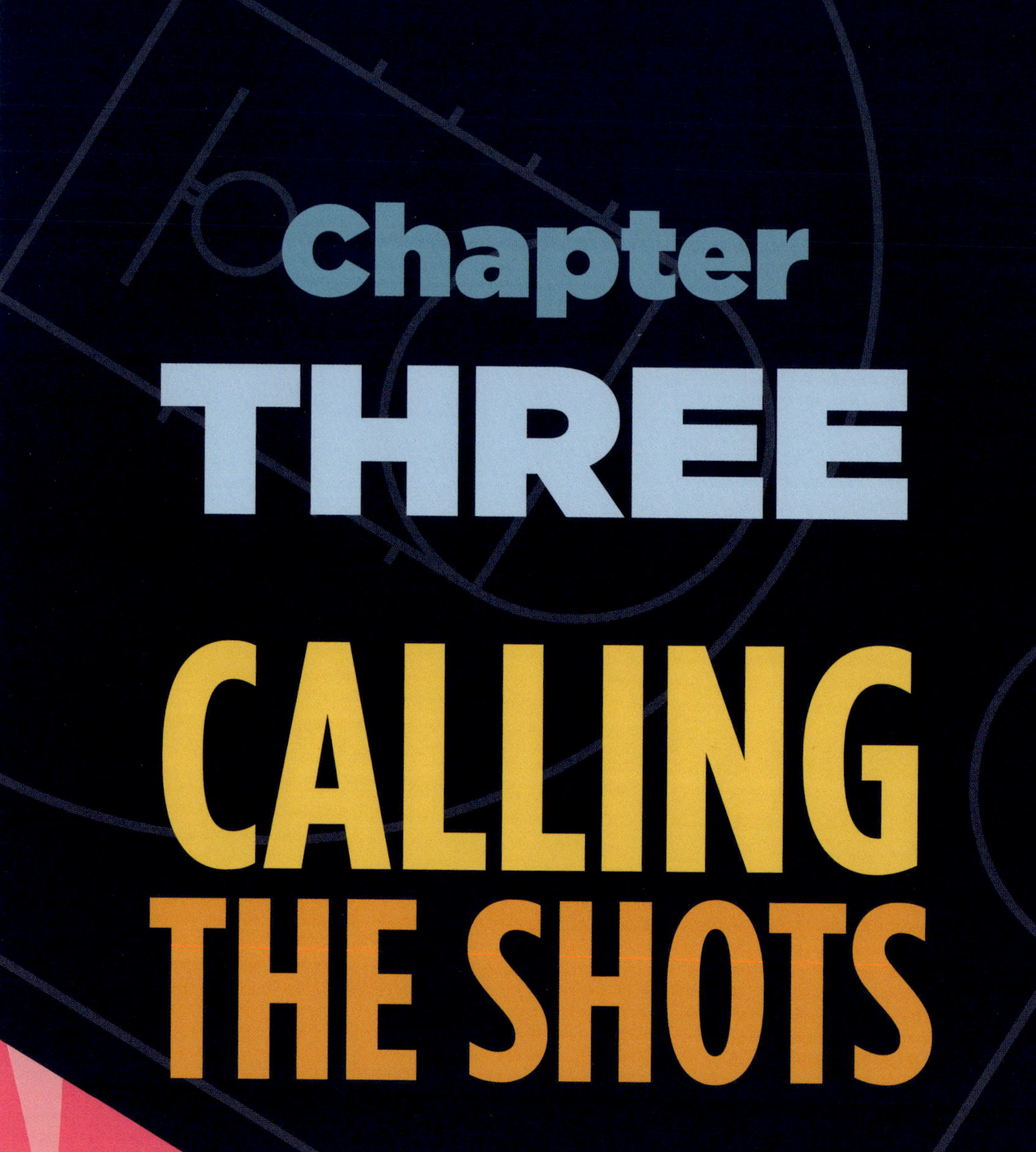

Chapter THREE

CALLING THE SHOTS

When the Utah Starzz played their first game, head coach Denise Taylor was at the helm. Taylor had been the head coach at Northeastern Illinois University before the Starzz approached her to coach the **charter** WNBA team. After a disappointing season and a half, she was let go.

CHAPTER THREE

Over the years and the moves between the cities, the team went through ten head coaches. Dan Hughes had the longest **tenure**, spending eleven seasons with the team in San Antonio. But with the move to Las Vegas, the team wanted new leadership.

The Aces' first coach in their new home was former NBA player Bill Laimbeer. Laimbeer led the team to three playoff appearances. But after the 2021 season, he decided to step down from coaching.

Laimbeer's exit opened the door for Becky Hammon. She brought a lot of experience to the job, having previously played for both the San Antonio Stars and the New York Liberty. Coming to the Aces from the San Antonio Spurs, she was also the first full-time female assistant coach in NBA history.

FAST FACT

Becky Hammon became the highest-paid coach in the WNBA when the Aces hired her in 2022 with a salary of $1 million per year.

And that wasn't all. Hammon was also the first female coach in the NBA Summer League. In 2020, she was the first woman to take over as head coach in a regular season NBA game when the male coach was **ejected**.

Since joining the Aces in 2022, Hammon has led the team to two championships. "It shouldn't be easy. It should be hard as heck to go in there and repeat, and it was," she said on *SportsCenter* after the second championship in 2023. Hammon and the Aces proved that hard work, **resilience**, and teamwork pay off.

Calling the Shots

The Aces won back-to-back championships with coach Becky Hammon.

Chapter FOUR

QUEENS OF THE COURT

The Aces' mascot Bucket$ was named WNBA Mascot of the Year in 2022.

The Aces have been fortunate since moving to Las Vegas. They have fared well in the WNBA Draft, adding many talented players. Each one has brought her own skill set to the team.

CHAPTER FOUR

The Aces chose A'ja Wilson as their first-round pick in 2018. Wilson was a standout player at the University of South Carolina, where she led that team to a national championship. In her first year with the Aces, she was named **Rookie** of the Year and made the All-Star Team. On July 8, 2024, Wilson became the Aces all-time leading scorer. She represented the USA at the Olympics twice, in Tokyo in 2021 and in Paris in 2024, bringing home gold medals both times. Wilson was named WNBA MVP for the third time on September 22, 2024.

Kelsey Plum was another first-round draft pick. She joined the team in 2017 and made the WNBA All-Rookie Team. Each year, the top five rookie players in the league receive this honor. Plum was also named the MVP of the 2022 All-Star Game. She joined Wilson on Team USA at the Paris Olympics in 2024.

Guard Kelsey Plum is a three-time WNBA All-Star.

CHAPTER FOUR

Chelsea Gray joined the Aces in 2021, after playing for the Connecticut Sun and the Los Angeles Sparks. She won a championship with the Sparks in 2016. She was also part of the 2022 Aces championship team. In an interview with *Essence* magazine, she said, "We brought the first professional championship here in Las Vegas. And being a part of history, you are able to write your name that you are a part of making history, and I think that's pretty cool."

The Aces are a young team, but they have a long history in the WNBA. Their roots are in the original eight teams, but there have been many changes over the years. They rolled the dice and came up winning.

FAST FACT

Chelsea Gray was named WNBA Finals MVP in 2022.

GLOSSARY

adversity
Great difficulty

center
A basketball player who plays near the basket, often the tallest member of the team

charter
Having been part of a league or other group from the time of its establishment

ejected
Forced to leave an event such as a game, usually due to unacceptable conduct

forward
A basketball player who plays near the basket, often rebounding and scoring points

guard
A basketball player who focuses on passing, dribbling, and setting up plays

literacy
The ability to read and write

resilience
The ability to keep going despite tough challenges

revitalized
Inspired as if given new life

rookie
An athlete playing her first season as a member of a professional sports team

roster
A list of players on a sports team

tenure
Length of time serving in a job or position

SLAM DUNK WNBA TRIVIA

- Valued at $140 million in 2024, the Las Vegas Aces are worth more than any other WNBA team.
- The team plays its home games at the Michelob Ultra Arena in the Mandalay Bay Resort and Casino.
- The Aces mascot is Bucket$, a black-tailed jackrabbit. He is based on a real species found in the Mojave Desert.
- In 2023, Candace Parker became the first WNBA player to win a championship with three different teams. In addition to the title she won with the Aces, she won championships while playing for the Chicago Sky in 2021 and the Los Angeles Sparks in 2016.
- In 2024, the Aces became the first WNBA team to sell out the regular season.
- Football legend Tom Brady is a minority owner of the Aces.

FIND OUT MORE

IN PRINT

Davidson, B. Keith. *WNBA*. Crabtree Publishing, 2022.

Hill, Anne E. *Inside the Las Vegas Aces*. Lerner Publications, 2023.

Mooney, Carla. *New York Liberty*. Mitchell Lane Publishing, 2026.

ON THE INTERNET

Las Vegas Aces.
https://aces.wnba.com.

"Las Vegas Aces," ***ESPN*****, n.d.**
www.espn.com/wnba/team/_/name/lv/las-vegas-aces.

"Las Vegas Aces," ***FOX Sports*****, n.d.**
www.foxsports.com/wnba/las-vegas-aces-team.

INDEX

About the Author

Kerry Kelaher Fredeen lives in Hollywood, California. She has written several books for young readers. When she's not busy writing, she works at a Southern California library. Her love of sports began as a child, watching games with her dad in New Jersey.